PEACE

PEACE

Emily Hunter Slingluff

Front Cover by Karen Woodard,
Virginia Beach, Virginia

Printed in the United States of America
CreateSpace, an Amazon.com.Co

ISBN-13: 9781516802289
ISBN 10: 1516802284
First edition, November 2015
Second edition, January 2017, Revised

Other books by Emily Hunter Slingluff

A Present to the Newborn,
1987
also published as
A Primer for Positive Parenting

Parenting Without Punishment,
2013

CHAPTERS

1

FOR EVERY PROBLEM,
THERE IS A SOLUTION

Many years ago, when my husband and I were having a house built by a very nice contractor, there was a glitch. Something had gone wrong and I was a bit upset. But the contractor, Mr. Hap Hoy, said to me, "For every problem, there is a solution." Those words ring in my ears and have been repeated by me, over the years, as I have smiled instead of frowned over various glitches with workmen and others. Don't those words make you smile now, just thinking that?

Writing this, I just thought why his nickname must have been Hap. That was not his real name, but everybody called him Hap. He was hap - py. He was happy with life and therefore thinking positively about solving any problems, rather than thinking negatively about doing nothing to help solve a problem.

Maybe Hap's words somehow influenced me to tackle writing this.

2

IS PEACE POSSIBLE?

What is peace? It is the opposite of war. It is the opposite of unkindness. Imagine the world full of people who all care about each other. That is peace.

Right now, there are many individuals who are peaceful. So, if peace is present anywhere, then spreading it is surely possible.

When you read or hear about a mass murder in a school or in a church or anywhere, or about a single murder, or about a business man or anybody being dishonest, or about a child being unkind to another child, and some people are saying why oh why, what do you think? Do you think it is a big mystery? Or do you think it is not really a mystery?

Louis Machado wrote in THE RIGHT TO BE INTELLIGENT that "the world can be no better than the people in it." So, as we look at the problems of crime and meanness at all levels and if we want to help change crime and meanness to peacefulness and kindness, we can, first of all, remember that crimes are committed by individuals and meanness is expressed by individuals. We do not need to throw up our hands in exasperation, saying this is too complicated. We are not dealing with a cloud called crime. We are dealing with human beings. Individual people are the problem and the solution.

Why are some people dishonest, unlawful, or mean in other ways? Why do some people want to take away the lives of others? There really seems to be an answer to these questions and a solution to the problem.

The answer is not poverty or race or our schools. Aren't we all tired of hearing some people say that the problem is race? Name any race. Is everybody in that race unlawful and uncaring about others? Certainly not. Or is everybody in that race law abiding and caring about others? Certainly not. How about the reason for meanness and dishonesty being poverty? Are all poor people unkind to each other and lashing out at the rest of the world? Certainly not. Are all poor people kind and honest? Certainly not. Are all wealthy people unlawful and mean? Certainly not. Are all wealthy people kind and honest? Certainly not. Individuals, whether poor or rich, and whether from any race we can name, not only vary in personality, but some are kind and caring while others are unkind and wanting to lash out.

Many very kind people are very poor. And they are law abiding. Poverty matters, but it is not the primary reason for people being mean to each other. And that is the topic here. Peace and meanness are sort of opposites.

Maybe I am daring to write about this huge and important topic because I graduated from Sweet Briar College where we learned that anything is possible! As I write this, in the summer of 2015, the news is just out that something many Sweet Briar alumnae expected, but some others thought impossible, has happened. The president of the college announced in March that the college could not survive and it would close in August, this year. However, this is what happened. Some alumnae immediately started working, believing that anything is possible, and tried legally and financially and emotionally and intelligently to change what the president of the college had announced. Yesterday, about three months after the president's sudden and firm announcement that Sweet Briar would close forever, the news came out that the president and board of directors of the college are resigning and letting others who want to save the college take over. The college is not closing now after all. How many people in this world would have done what some caring alumnae and others associated with the college believed was possible? The word, "can't," probably did not enter the minds of those who have worked so hard and have succeeded in this task. The new president of the college has suggested the slogan, AT SWEET BRIAR COLLEGE, THE IMPOSSIBLE IS JUST ANOTHER PROBLEM TO SOLVE. So maybe it was in those four years at Sweet Briar College that I was influenced a lot and sort of taught that anything is possible, so that all these many years later, I am daring to write about peace, a topic that may seem untouchable.

However, while schools matter a lot, they are not the main problem or the main solution. You know why. When students, whether in elementary school, high school, college or beyond, are being influenced, each person accepts the influences differently because the influences are being received by human beings who were influenced already in different ways. While every single influence in life matters for as long as we live, we know that the influences are building on other influences as we age.

In this case of trying to promote peace, we can realize that first, we can identify a major cause of unkindness at any level, including a school bully to a mass murderer; and only after that, the solution to the problem. Then, we will be closer to peace.

3

THE WORLD CAN
BE NO BETTER
THAN THE PEOPLE IN IT

As Machado wrote, the world can be no better than the people in it. We know that people have different personalities, different degrees of intelligence, and abilities in various fields. We surely appreciate that. There is something else that every single person can have. If all people had it, there would be more kindness and lawfulness. That is happiness.

A very respected psychiatrist said to me:

"Happiness
is the goal of psychiatrists
in treating patients of any age."

Crimes are rarely committed by happy people who respect others because they themselves are happy with life instead of confused, insecure, and unhappy with life.

At this time, there have been numerous, very publicized, mass murders in this country. Often those committing the murders seem to want to be called terrorists. Maybe not all do, but some. Perhaps anyone who chooses to commit big crimes could, instead, be termed a weakling? Certainly a mean person is hardly a truly strong soul, but is suffering from confusion and unhappiness and therefore, weakness.

If we want to have more peace instead of more crimes and meanness, if we want more people caring about each other rather than wanting to hurt each other, then we want more people who are happy instead of unhappy.

We can do this by helping parents remember their importance, particularly in the formative years of their child's life, and by helping parents remember the importance of their child being happy with life instead of unhappy. Also parents can remember the importance of being on the child's side rather than on some opposing side. This can be called parentogethering, a word I made up.

Again, the world can be no better than the people in it. Every parent can help make people better.

4

DELVING

So far, this is not complicated, and it is not complicated as we continue to delve. Are there other options to helping promote more peace, whether between individuals, in families, or neighborhoods, or all over?

1) Have a magic wand touch everybody? Not happening!

2) Send all people to counseling, to therapy, and then all people will be full of inner peace? Send all 30 and 40 year olds and all 50 and 60 year olds, and all 20 years old, too, and all 10 year olds? Would that

work? It is very difficult to change a person and often impossible. Counseling can help, but changing all people of all ages to what they could have been is not happening either. As social reformer Frederick Douglass said, many years ago, "It is easier to build strong children than to repair broken men."

So, let's try to get it right in the beginning. The formative years of life are called formative for a reason. They are formative. And who is the main influence in those early years? The parent. The parent makes the decisions or allows the influences on the brand new baby and toddler.

Probably most parents do try to help their child be the best he or she can be and still many children grow up confused and insecure and, therefore, so unhappy with life that they hurt themselves or others in small or huge ways. This is probably not the fault of the parents as much as it is the fault of what has been taught to the parents as the best way to parent. The good news is that the parenting philosophy that was most prevalent in this country a generation ago has been changing. For a long time, many parents were led to believe that the parent-child relationship should be a sort of dictatorship. Surely it works better if the parent helps the child learn by being on the same side with the child, rather than sort of against the child. Through parentogethering, the parent can easily help the child be happy to be alive.

5

THAT WORD: HAPPY

Over the past years since my first book came out, I have asked many people what they want for their child. I ask people from all sorts of backgrounds, different lifestyles, poor, wealthy, different ages, and even, more than once, have asked groups of parents who had abused their children. I ask parents and grandparents and people of all ages who do not even have children what they think a parent should most want for the child.

What do you want your child to be when:

2 days old?
3 years old?
10 years old?
30 years old?
70 years old?

Without thinking deeply, some parents might quickly think that they want the 2 day old to sleep through the night! Or the 3 year old to be obedient and not ask so many questions! Or the 10 year old to be making good grades or be a sports star! Or the 30 year old to be making money! Or the 70 year old...what word?

Just suppose the child is one of the things named above or anything else a parent might think, but suppose also that that human being is unhappy with life. Now, what is the one word?

Those who are unhappy are more likely to want to lash out. Bullies in elementary school are obviously not happy because they want to hurt others, either physically or emotionally. To take this a step deeper, mass murderers are almost always unhappy people. Crimes at any level are usually committed by unhappy people. A major crime fighter in a large city in this country told me that he did not believe anybody he ever arrested for anything, small or large, could have been termed a happy soul.

Robert Browning, the well-known English poet, wrote "Oh, make us happy and you make us good."

A parent just asking the child to care about others helps. But suppose that same parent orders the child around and punishes the child for the slightest imperfections and just generally makes life for the child unpleasant, tending to put the child on edge all the time. Will that child be happy and therefore, good? Not as likely as would be the child of the parent who, instead, works with the child instead of against the child, talking with the child about anything in the whole wide world and also listening and discussing and reasoning instead of dictating, and above all, respecting the child as a worthy human being. Oh wow, that child would be different from the other one.

Just saying, "be nice" is a good thing for a parent to say to the child, but falls on confused ears if the parent is not nice all the time to the child! Don't we all know that? Suppose the parent does not try to think of some way to punish a child for some human imperfection, but instead communicates with the child. Communicating works so much better than punishing. For this to work, the parent can replace rules with guidelines. All of us are imperfect. We make mistakes, often unintentionally. So, a rule is likely to be broken and where rules are present, there must be punishment if a rule is broken or there will be chaos. So, instead, rules can be replaced by guidelines. Then, a child not following some guideline will not have to be punished. The consequence of not following a guideline can be wonderful communication! That means talking and listening and explaining and talking and reasoning and listening some more. That makes the parent-child relationship wonderful, fun, one side instead of two opposing sides.

Well, what about a child whose parent acted like a dictator, who treated the child with sternness and meanness? Suppose that child, as he matures, is obviously insecure and confused and unhappy? That is not what I am writing about here except to thank the many people who work alone or in organizations to try to undo the harms that have already been done to children as they have grown. This writing is to try to lessen the need for such remedial organizations. This writing is to encourage a way of parenting that will lessen the need for trying to undo what the parent had done in the formative years. However, there is always hope, too, that a child who has been mistreated by the parent can have her or his outlook on life changed if the parent makes a change in parenting philosophy and tells the child, clearly, carefully, strongly, that this is happening. A parent can find a quiet time to sit with the child and say she or he is changing her or his way of parenting to a way where they are both open with each other. A parent can say that there will not be rules, but guidelines, so not punishment but communication. The parent can say she or he wants to be the child's side and is sorry for not being that way from the beginning. Hopefully, there is always hope! Right? Clearly, it is up to the parent to take such an option if it becomes needed. A child can only hope for such.

It is thrilling to me to find that this way of parentogethering is becoming so much more prevalent than it seemed to be years ago. Need it be said that if every single parent treated every single child with respect from the moment that little human being came into the world, there would be less need for so many people and organizations that are trying to undo the harms of what parents did to children when they were in those formative years? Is there a living soul who disagrees with that statement?

6

IT TAKES A PARENT,
NOT A VILLAGE

So, realizing the importance of a parent helping a child be happy, sort of exactly what can a parent do? In Plato's *Republic,* Socrates says (in translation,) "the beginning is the most important part of any work." If we agree that we want to have more people who care about each other, that is a first step. Then, we can realize that the beginning of life matters. And then we can realize that it is easy for a parent to influence a newborn and toddler in the important formative years in a positive way to make him or her happy to be alive, in spite of almost anything else.

Genes matter, but new scientific studies show that even genes in little babies can be changed if there is physical or emotional abuse to the child by the parent. Also, regardless of genes, we know that environment matters.

We know that everything that happens to a little baby is important in that baby's emotional development. All we need do is put ourselves in the other person's place if we wonder about that. We can imagine being a baby, lying in a crib and wondering what is going on. Where am I? What is this? Where is that person who just put me here? And then, making a sound in hopes that the person will come help me, talk with me, and above all, hold me. Making a cry is the only way a baby can communicate in the beginning. If a parent wants to have good communication with her or his child, that parent clearly should start in the beginning. The parent absolutely should respond to the newborn's plea for help. Good communication between parent and child hardly works well if off to a bad start. It can be good later in life if the parent tries hard to undo what might have been a bad start, but it is so easy if the parent answers the baby from the beginning.

For too many years, we read and heard from many people that when a baby cries, don't worry. We were told not to go to that baby because then the baby would be spoiled! It is worth writing in large letters: GO TO THE BABY WHO CRIES. And, as Dr. T. Berry Brazelton, head of the Brazelton Institute, in Boston, wrote in the margin of my second book about parenting when I sent it to him for approval, "then find out what the baby wants." I like the words of the famous Dr. Brazelton. He is emphasizing that the baby is asking. The little baby is communicating the only way a baby can talk. If the parent wants to have good communication, then surely the parent should answer the baby. If a parent is worried about spoiling the baby, and spoiled means ruined we know, then be sure that NOT going to a little baby who is asking for help the only way he or she can ask, is the way to spoil (ruin) that child. How would we feel if we were the baby and nobody came to help us when we asked? We would feel confused, sad, and unloved. If, instead, the parent goes to the baby who is communicating the only way he or she can communicate, then how would we feel, if we were the baby? We would feel loved, secure, respected, loved, and happy. A parent cannot hold a baby too much. A parent can take the baby where she or he is doing something and continue to hold the baby or at least put the baby where the parent is doing something. This attention to the baby when that little newborn is first discovering the world matters so much. A parent cannot hold a baby too much. It gives the baby a feeling of security that will last.

Is this enough said? Is it necessary to go on and on about the parent continuing to answer the child through the years? That matters too.

Is it necessary to say that the parent should continue to respect the child at every age? If we respect another human being, we answer that human being. Oh too often, we have read that the child must respect the parent, that this is so important. But if the parent wants the child to grow up feeling secure and confident and happy with life, then should not the parent also treat the child as a human being worthy of respect, from the moment of its birth? Some parents may just wish their teenager or adult child had self-confidence, not even realizing that the parent could have easily instilled self-confidence in the child by treating the child with respect. It makes the child happy with life and therefore, more self-confident rather than confused and insecure and yes, unhappy.

Surely the parent who wants to truly help her or his child should answer that child when a newborn in the crib and when a toddler learning so much about life all the time, and when a teenager, too, learning what the parent chooses to discuss which should be anything at all. Why not? Who said the parent and child cannot be good friends, even best friends? I find more people finally accepting the fact that such a relationship is as wonderful as any relationship can possibly be!

Perhaps this is the place to write again that neither poverty nor race nor schools are the main cause of meanness and crime. Do we not all know some very poor people who are so kind and caring that it is almost hard to believe?

Recently, a man told me that he grew up in a house where there was sometimes no food at all available. His mother had very little money. But he said that his mother explained everything to him and talked with him and made it very clear that she cherished him so much. He was, and is, so happy with life and he says that his mother is the reason.

Another great example is Naomi Griffith, author of *Parenting from the Heart,* who I heard speak in Norfolk, Virginia in 1988 and who said she grew up extremely poor and that "when people think that poor people can't help cherish their children, I resent it."

Every influence in life does matter and this includes a lack of money or sometimes too much money, and it includes race and it includes school teachers, and everything. But it would be silly to overlook the importance of the formative years when a baby's outlook on life is being formed by the parent either directly or indirectly through the influences the parent chooses or allows. True, deep happiness or the opposite is being instilled in the formative years whether the parent realizes it or not.

Of course no child will be perfect as no adult is perfect. Only in striving for perfection will we come closer to it, but we should remember that none of us will be perfect.

While delving more, we should recognize the fact that one parent can be a super fine parent. Sure, two loving parents is great, but whether by death or divorce or whatever, if there is only one parent, that one can help the child be the best he or she can be. Let's all stop thinking that being a single parent is an excuse for having a child who is confused and unhappy. One parent can be kind and caring and on the child's side, rather than on some opposing side. And, perhaps a strange note to add here, but true... if there is only one parent, that parent's philosophy does not have to be tempered with another's. Sometimes, two parents have different parenting philosophies so the child is treated differently by each parent. Not knowing of any scientific study about the usual results of this scenario, it seems that having one parent who is kind and open with the child, who works with the child, on the same side, is all important. Happiness and security about one's place in this world, if instilled by two parents or by one parent, is likely to help the child be able to withstand almost whatever else happens to him or her forever.

Although a book was written called *It Takes a Village*, it is surely more accurate to say that IT TAKES A PARENT because:

1. Imagine a child who lives in a wonderful village, a town where most of the town people are nice and friendly and caring about children and adults, too, where churches pay attention to children and have special meetings for them, and where there are no gangs or meanies ready to pounce

on children. BUT, when the child in that village walks into his own house, his parent is on drugs and calls out to the child that he is a few minutes late coming home and therefore is going to be punished by going to his room without any food for the rest of the day. Where the parent is mean to the child, perhaps calling him a no-good boy for not doing what he was supposed to do, and saying that she wishes she did not have him as a son. Of course, there are variations to this scenario. Some are much worse than this, involving beating and worse, and some are softer, but still dictatorial or disrespectful or even just unpleasant.

2. Then, imagine a child who lives in a village where crime is rampant, where most residents keep their doors locked and are afraid to go out on the street at night, where there are no churches or

community centers that try to help children, where there are not even any recreation areas. BUT, the parent of the child who lives in such a village is kind always to the child. The parent makes it clear that she or he cares about the child and is interested in what he or she is thinking or learning. The parent listens and discusses anything, everything. The parent works with the child as the parent teaches, not against the child as if the parent-child relationship were some sort of master-slave relationship. Imagine the happiness of that child.

I think it takes a parent.

7

YOUR REACTION

Now repeating the question near the beginning of this writing. When you read about a mass murder in a school or in a church or anywhere, or about a business man being dishonest, or about a child being mean to another child, what do you think? Do you think it is a big mystery or not?

Perhaps you are thinking that there does seem to be an answer to the question of why some people lash out at others in small or big ways, why some people even murder people they have never known or murder people close to them. And perhaps you are thinking that there is a solution. And maybe you are thinking, or have always thought, that we, as parents, can try to help make people happier with life, one parent and one child at a time; and in doing this, help more people live in peace.

Or maybe you are wondering if one parent helping one child be happy is significant in the big picture? Perhaps we should consider here the words of President John F. Kennedy, "Those who make peaceful revolution impossible will make violent revolution inevitable." The dictionary defines revolution as change. Certainly change takes place in life for many reasons and change is likely to continue. But do changes need to be violent? Many years ago, the Rev. Martin Luther King, Jr, knew of a big change taking place in the United States and he became famous for advocating peaceful change. President Kennedy's words are thought provoking in any relationship,

whether the relationship is between individuals or within families or other
groups or even between nations. Actually
we know that nations do not make decisions. People in nations make decisions.

Yes, this is a big topic. But not as baf-
fling once examined?

8

WHY WRITE THIS

maybe just to clarify all of this for myself. Starting a few months after my marriage, I started studying parenting, watching how parents treated their children and how their children treated them back. The whole parenting thing became clear. Parents matter so much, I realized.

And the big picture of humanity and wars being fought and then the people in the nations fighting against each other becoming good friends after the wars were over had always puzzled me. Were the wars necessary really? Maybe so, I wondered. Or maybe not, I wondered. Having lived through World War II as a child, I remember keeping quiet during supper time with my family as we listened to the news about the war on the radio. We had relatives and friends who were being killed. I remember that after the war, people in this country became friends again with the Germans and the Japanese, who had been our "enemies." Even then, I wondered. What do you think? Killing to achieve peace? Sort of like a parent being mean to the child so that the child will grow up to be kind?

People killing each other seems mean. It seems wrong. It seems clear that it is both mean and wrong. People hurting each other in any way seems mean and wrong. Many years ago, I told my little son that it seemed right not to hit back if anybody ever hit him. I said to feel sorry for the person who did the hitting because that little person probably had learned about hitting because he had been hit, and perhaps by his own parent. That is sad.

Anyway, this has been a lifelong study for me, as probably for many. I hope that, somehow, this little writing will promote fewer questions about why crime exists on many levels. What to do about the existing crime and meanness is a topic I am not tackling now. Many fine people are trying to deal with what is already present, but it is difficult to change what already exists. I am trying to reduce the need for remedial programs by presenting thoughts about the importance of every parent trying to help every child appreciate life, and, by saying that what a lot of parents did and some still do, which is having a dictator-like relationship with the child, can so happily be replaced by parentogethering.

For too long, too many parents have been told, and have believed, that parenting is a big problem full of smaller problems of all sorts at all ages. I strongly believe, I know really, that parenting need not be a problem, but can be an enormous pleasure all the time. Some may respond to that statement by saying, oh you just had a different kind of child or different children. My response is that all children are different. Every one. Every one of us is different. But believe me, every single child, no matter what, responds to obvious love from the parent, to being held a lot when a baby, to being respected at every single age from babyhood to teenage years and beyond, and to having open communication with the parent about anything in life.

I have worked hard writing three books about parenting, the first one more detailed and the second one only three points for parents, to make parenting clear and easy. Parenting need not be complicated or difficult. This one is probably written because I have heard too many people say... why do you think that person murdered those people? And, because too often I listen to a webinar or read a book about parenting and find that the author or the leader of any group talking about parenting is assuming that parenting is full of problems. It sort of breaks my heart. Parenting a problem? What a sad thought. It can be one of the greatest pleasures in the whole world. And I am not the only person who knows this. We just want more to know.

A baby who feels loved and comforted and happy is a pleasure beyond pleasure. If the parent does not want to enjoy parenting, then why oh why have a baby at all? Birth control is available. Or giving away a baby for adoption by someone who wants a child is an option. My greatest wish in life, beyond personal wishes, is that no unwanted child be born in the world. The world does not need unhappy, confused people added to the population.

Maybe more books need to be written that say parents should stop reading books about parenting and instead just start doing what comes naturally which is love love love that little person. Enjoy that baby, toddler, teenager, and adult and consider parentogethering. Parents can produce peace.

SUMMARY

(Hoy, Machado, Douglass, Browning, Kennedy)

"For every problem, there is a solution."

"The world can be no better than the people in it."

"It is easier to build strong children than to repair broken men."

"Oh make us happy and you make us good."

"Those who make peaceful revolution impossible will make violent revolution inevitable."

PERSONAL ADDENDUM

It seems strange to me to be writing about peace without mentioning God. Can true, deep, happiness in life exist without believing in Him would be the question here, but because I do believe, it is impossible for me to know. Counting on God, talking with Him, thinking of Him all make me cry tears of happiness. Still, having lived for so long and having read and looked and listened, it seems that happiness in a person can exist with other beliefs.

The present head of a large national organization trying to help children did tell me that she was abused as a child and abandoned when fourteen years old. She said that she only survived by finding inner peace because she learned to rely on God.

Different opinions exist on this deep and important topic. But probably all who think about how to help people live together more peacefully do agree that every parent's words and actions with every child, particularly in the beginning, matter forever, not only to that one child, but to everybody that child touches forever.

ACKNOWLEDGEMENTS

Cover. Mahatma Ghandi, "If we are to teach real peace in this world, we shall have to begin with the children."

p.9. Nancy Hoy, wife of Hap Hoy permission to quote him

p.11. Definition of peace, *Webster's New International Dictionary of the English Language*

p.12. and title of Chapter 3 Louis Machado, from *The Right To Be Intelligent*, "The world can be no better than the people in it."

p.15. "At Sweet Briar College, the impossible is just another problem to solve." 2015, Phillip C. Stone, president of Sweet Briar College

p.22. Frederick Douglass in 1855 "It is easier to build strong children than to repair broken men."

p.27. Robert Browning, 19th cen. English poet, "Oh make us happy and you make us good"

p.34. Abuse Casts A Long Shadow by Changing Children's Genes, Eleanor Nelsen, Oct. 2014, Nova

p.35. Dr. T. Berry Brazelton

p.39. Naomi Griffith, author of *Parenting from the Heart*

p.41. *It Takes A Village*, by Hillary Clinton

p.46. Definition of revolution, *Webster's New International Dictionary of the English Language*

p.46. John F, Kennedy, President of USA, 1961-1963 "Those who make peaceful revolution impossible will make violent revolution inevitable."

p.59. Stephanie Mann, head of SafeKidsNow.com, a nationwide organization to support and strengthen families

Chauncey Prigmore, II, helpful formatting

Emily Harkins Filer, chaplain and former head of Lee's Friends, reading and helping

James Holmes, Children's Harbor, reading and helping so much with agreement

Douglass Mackall, III, reading and editing

Dr. T. Berry Brazelton, head of The Brazelton Institute, Boston, MA

Many at CreateSpace, with everything

And others

Thank you so much.

www.ingramcontent.com/pod-product-compliance
Lightning Source LLC
Chambersburg PA
CBHW070322290526
45791CB00003B/1216